SAVE THE MANATEES
WITH MOM AND ME

Catherine Elizabeth Davis

Save the Manatees with Mom and Me

Copyright © 2021 by Catherine Elizabeth Davis

First Edition

ISBN-13: 978-1-7365197-0-7

Designed by:
creativgraphics.com

To my sons, Christopher and Elijah, and to all the children who like manatees

My favorite animals
Are manatees!
Although known as "sea cows,"
They swim with great ease.

They eat mostly plants,
So they're called **herbivores**.
And they are the creatures
My mom most adores!

They swim in the river
And all through the bay.
Alone or in pairs –
Manatees find their way!

Calm and **defenseless**,
They're quite gentle creatures.
I sure like the look
Of their interesting features.

Manatees are not
Related to whales,
Despite heavy weights
And flat, paddle-like tails.

They have egg-shaped heads
And such wrinkly faces.
They live in **subtropic**
And **tropical** places.

I'll never forget
The first one that I saw.
So graceful and stunning –
Not one single **flaw**!

That manatee grazed
On weeds and eelgrass.
It ate a lot to keep
Its large body **mass**!

I loved its unique color –
A brownish-gray.
I got so excited
When it swam my way!

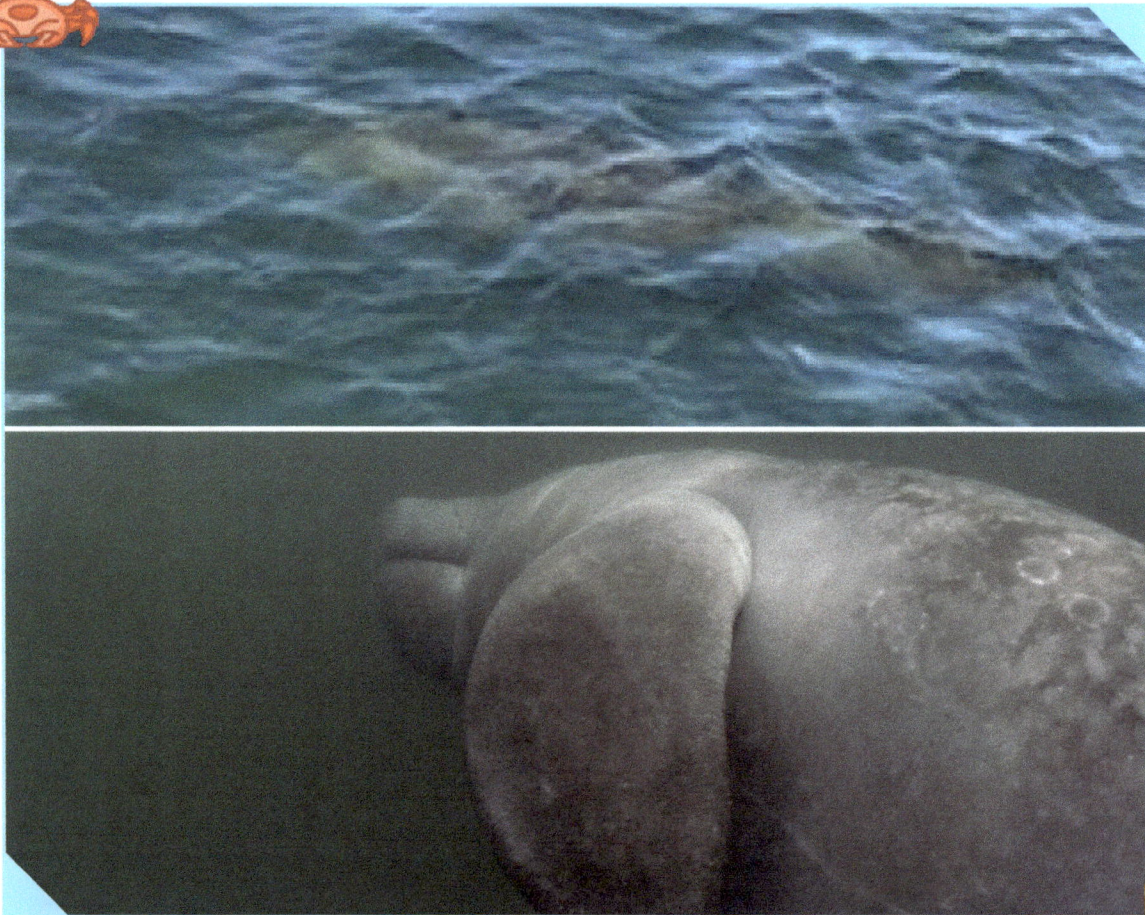

It slowly approached me
To come check me out.
I felt so adventurous –
Just like a boy scout!

I gazed at the manatee's
Small, peaceful eye.
It was so amazing;
Mom started to cry!

The sight of the manatee
Brought us great cheer.
Although it was large,
We had nothing to fear.

Mom said they're **threatened** –
She showed me a list
Of **species** that sadly
Might cease to exist!

I realized something then,
So suddenly.
They need our help –
Help from you and from me!

Common Name	Scientific Name	Status
Macaque, Toque	*Macaca sinica*	Threatened
Manatee, Amazonian	*Trichechus inunguis*	Endangered
Manatee, West African	*Trichechus senegalensis*	Threatened
Manatee, West Indian	*Trichechus manatus*	Threatened
Mandrill	*Mandrillus (=Papio) sphinx*	Endangered

My mother and I
Together agreed:
We must work to save
Every last manatee!

We started to travel
To so many places,
To run and support
The great manatee races!

We pick up the garbage
And clean up the beach.
To save the manatees,
Trash must be out of reach!

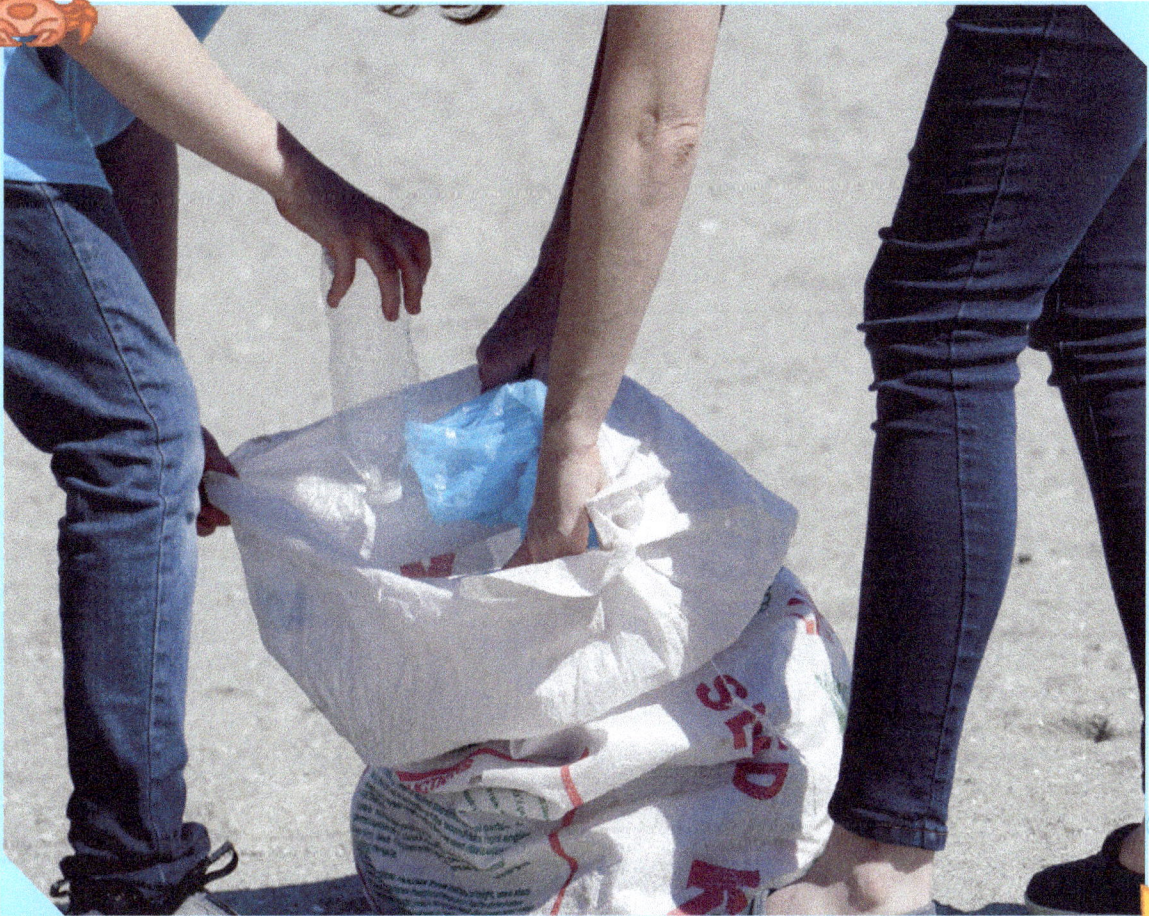

I love **volunteering**
At different events
And sharing brochures
Under canopied tents.

Manatees

Educational Guide

Raising
Public Awareness

**"Together We Can
Make A Difference!"**

We drive our boat slowly
And most carefully,
So that we don't hit them –
Not one manatee!

They are "gentle giants,"
And that is a plus.
We'll never hurt them,
And they'll never hurt us!

These "floating potatoes"
Are so very sweet.
I love every manatee
That I can meet!

I think of the manatees
As my dear friends.
I add pictures to letters
That my mom sends.

Save the Manatees
Help them to survive!

We help out the manatees
With all we do.
And if you love manatees,
You can help, too!

We need these great **mammals**,
As I'm sure you see.
Join us and we can
Save each manatee!

THE END

Save the "Chubby Mermaids"

Why? Manatees play a very important role to our ecosystem. Manatees eat a large amount of seagrass and other plants that could block our waterways. This helps to control mosquitos and overgrowth of invasive plant species. Manatees' deaths are mostly related to human activity.

Clean Up Look and Find

Help save the manatees by cleaning up the beach.

FIND

4 Straws
2 Plastic bags
3 Bottle caps
1 Glass bottle
4 Forks
3 Beverage cans
5 Fishing lines
4 Cigarette butts
1 Tire

29

Organizations/Rescue Centers That Help Manatees

If you are interested in supporting, donating, or adopting a manatee or see a manatee in distress, below is a list of different organizations/rescue centers that help manatees.

1. Save The Manatee Club

533 Versailles Dr, Suite 100

Maitland, FL 32751

1-800-432-5646/407-539-0990

2. Dolphin Research Center

Licensed Florida Keys Manatee

Rescue Team

Grassy Key, FL

www.dolphins.org

3. Amazon Rescue Center

Centro de Rescate Amazonico-CREA

www.centroderescateamazonico.com

Glossary

defenseless - being without defense or protection

flaw - a mark or imperfection

herbivores - animals that eat plants

mammals - warm-blooded animals that have vertebrae, usually have hair or fur, and feed their young with milk that the mother produces

mass - the amount or quantity of matter in an object

species - a group of similar organisms that can reproduce with each other

subtropic - areas bordering the tropics with hot summers and mild winters; nearly tropical

threatened - at risk of becoming endangered

tropical - hot and humid

volunteering - to offer to do something freely without being made or paid to do it

Photo Credits

Permission to use the following pictures and photographs is gratefully acknowledged and appreciated:

Animal Welfare Institute (AWI): graphic of a portion of the endangered species list (last updated January 2019), page 16

Daysha S. Brown, Pennsylvania: three photos of manatee splashing, page 27

Christopher Davis, SC: photos of manatees, page 12; manatee painting, page 24; author photo, page 33

Elijah Davis, SC: photos on pages 9 and 19

Alexandrea Deliere, Hunter Springs Kayaks and Manatee Tour & Dive, Fl: photos of manatees on front cover, pages 2, 7, 13, 14, 15, and back cover

Jessica Ingalls, FL: photos of manatees, pages 3, 5, and 6; manatees' tails, page 8; manatees, pages 11, 17, 22, 23, 25, and 26

References

Alina Bradford, Live Science Contributor (March 31,2017). Live Science: Manatees-Facts About Sea Cows. Retrieved from https://www.livescience.com/27405-manatees.html on January 17, 2021

Animal Welfare Institute: List of Endangered Species (Last updated January 2019). Retrieved from https://awionline.org/content/list-endangered-species on November 18, 2021

Emily Frost (March 31, 2014). Smithsonian Magazine: 14 Fun Facts About Manatees. Retrieved from https://www.smithsonianmag.com/science-nature/14-fun-facts-about-manatees-180950308/ on January 16, 2021

About The Author

Catherine Elizabeth Davis is a South Carolina licensed optician and holds a Bachelor of Arts degree from Coastal Carolina University. She is also author of the children's book *Do You Like Snakes*? and *The Adventures of Foxie the Doxie at the Beach*.

Born and raised in South Carolina, Catherine grew up with a love of animals and the outdoors. Her favorite marine animal is the manatee! This book is inspired by her oldest child, Christopher, after he saw a manatee for the first time and felt the need to help save them.

www.ingramcontent.com/pod-product-compliance
Lightning Source LLC
Chambersburg PA
CBHW041600260326
41914CB00011B/1337